A Puppy is Born

A Puppy is Born

by Heiderose & Andreas Fischer-Nagel

~ translated by Andrea Mernan ~

G. P. Putnam's Sons   New York

For our daughter Tamarica

We are especially thankful to Frau Lieselotte Wegner,
the owner of the dachshund from Thanerberg, who with her
friendship, love and unending energy helped us with
placing her dogs in the right light.

First American edition 1985
First published by Kinderbuchverlag Reich,
Lucerne, 1983, under the title
Ein Leben auf kurzen Beinen.
© 1983 by Kinderbuch Reich Luzern AG
English translation copyright © 1985 by G. P. Putnam's Sons
All rights reserved. Published simultaneously in Canada
by General Publishing Co., Limited, Toronto.
Printed in Hong Kong.   Designed by Alice Lee
Library of Congress Cataloging in Publication Data
Fischer-Nagel, Heiderose.   A puppy is born.
Translation of: Ein Leben auf kurzen Beinen.
Summary: Photographs and text portray the birth
and first few weeks of four wirehaired dachshunds.
1. Puppies—Juvenile literature. 2. Dogs—Parturition—
Juvenile literature. 3. Wirehaired dachshund—
Juvenile literature. [1. Wirehaired dachshund.
2. Dachshund. 3. Animals—Infancy]
I. Fischer-Nagel, Andreas. II. Title.
SF426.5.F5713 1985   636.7'53   85-3505
ISBN 0-399-21234-5
First impression

There are many different kinds of dogs and they do many different things. Some, like Seeing Eye dogs, are helpers. And some, like sheepdogs, are workers. But most are pets.

All dogs are related to the wolf even if many varieties no longer resemble it. The German shepherd looks a little like a wolf, but most dogs don't. They have changed and changed over time and now there are about four hundred different kinds of dogs.

Certain dogs are considered to be special because they're pedigreed. That means that they have been registered in a special book that gives information about their family history. It tells who their parents were, who their grandparents were, and sometimes it goes even further back than that. This way their owners can tell exactly what kind of dog they have. Max and Missy are both pedigreed dogs.

Max and Missy are wirehaired dachshunds. Missy, on the right, is going to have a litter of puppies and Max is the father. The puppies will be born in about two months. Already they are beginning to grow inside Missy.

At first, Missy doesn't look any different, but she does begin to eat more. After about a month, as the puppies get larger and larger inside her, Missy's stomach looks rounder and rounder.

Now it is a few days before the puppies will be born. Missy acts restless. She doesn't want to be left alone. This is a sure sign that the puppies are ready to be born.

All dogs like to pick the place where they are going to give birth. It might be in a cardboard box the family has prepared, or in the back of a closet, but Missy has chosen her familiar basket with its bright red pillows.

When Missy feels that the first puppy is ready to be born, she helps by pressing it out of the opening of her birth canal, which is just under her tail. As she does this, she lifts one of her hind legs and the puppy slides out, still enclosed in its fluid-filled birth sac. Most puppies are born with the head coming out first. But Missy's puppy has come out feet first. You can see him pressing against the sac, which Missy will break open when the puppy is out.

Missy licks her puppy clean and bites through the cord that connected the puppy to its mother while it was inside her. The puppy received nourishment through this cord before it was born. Missy is tired from the effort of giving birth to her first puppy.

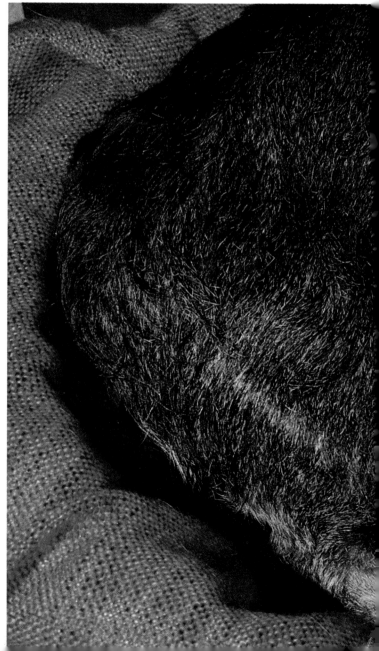

But there are still more puppies to come. Dogs usually have between four and six puppies, although some have as many as eight or more. When this happens, the puppies have to be bottle fed as well as nursed by the mother because the mother doesn't have enough milk to feed them all.

During the next hour, three more puppies are born. As soon as Missy licks them clean, they crawl to her tummy to suck warm milk from her nipples. Each puppy weighs about a half pound, which is about the same weight as two sticks of butter.

For the first few days, the puppies spend most of their time sleeping and eating. When the puppies are born, their eyes and their ears are tightly closed. For the first few weeks, they can't see, hear or smell so Missy helps them find her nipples by nudging them in the right direction. As soon as they find a nipple, they begin to suck.

The puppies sleep snuggled close together for warmth and comfort. After about ten days, their eyes begin to open, but even then they can't really see, or focus, properly. It will be about three weeks before this happens. They are able to smell a little earlier. After about two weeks, they sniff around their basket, exploring with their noses.

Within the first week, it is obvious that each puppy has its own personality. For example, one little female is quiet and shy while the other is lively and playful. One male, Charlie, is definitely more in charge than the other. He is quickly recognized as the leader of the litter. He snarls fiercely if someone tries to pet him, and Cocoa, his timid little sister, lets him bite her playfully.

When the puppies are about a month old, they begin to take care of themselves and stop depending so much on Missy. They also become less dependent on one another for security.

It won't be long before they will each be going off to a new home. But puppies adapt quickly to new homes so they won't be lonely for each other or Missy. But that is still a few weeks away. First they have to experience eating food from a bowl and going outside, where they will encounter more new things.

Here the puppies are outside with Missy. She stays close by as they visit the backyard for the first time. They romp in the cool, wet grass, sniffing at everything as they explore this sunny world filled with exciting smells.

Every day there is something new to experience. Today they have found bright, red bowls of food sitting in the grass. They sniff at it and paw it, trying to decide if it is something they should eat. Charlie and his brother dig in, but little Cocoa ignores her bowl and goes to Missy for some milk. Charlie, however, thinks his bowl is also a toy and he tries to drag it around with him all afternoon.

Their new diet makes the puppies even stronger and bolder. They scamper in the grass and snap at each other's noses, each one trying to outdo the other.

When they are not playing or exploring, the puppies rest quietly in the grass. But never for long. Today they are setting off to explore a small stream that trickles through a nearby field, Charlie leading the way.

The puppies find the stream and decide to take a drink. They crawl to the edge of the stream and plant their feet carefully on the bank before trying for their first sip. This isn't easy for a young puppy still learning how to keep its balance.

Puppies love to chew anything they can find, their bowls, a shoe, or a stick. Today, for the first time, they are chewing on a large bone. This starts a snarling tug-of-war between Charlie and his brother.

The puppies are two months old now, and it's almost time for them to go to their new homes. First, they are taken to the veterinarian for shots that will prevent them from getting any serious dog diseases.

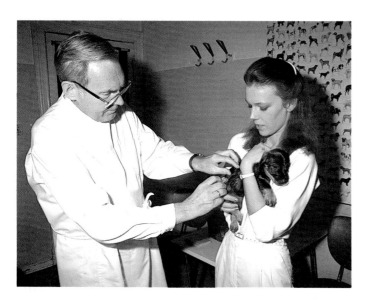 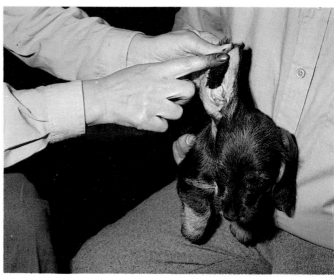

While they are there, the vet tattoos a number on the inside of their ears and dyes it black. This number can be used for identification if the dog is ever lost and will be recorded in the family history. Now the young puppies are ready to leave their mother. They are independent, healthy and big enough to live in a new home with a new owner.

Here is Cocoa in her new home. Already she has found a friend who loves her and wants to take care of her. Owning a dog is fun, but it is a lot of work too. Cocoa must be fed the right food, get plenty of play and exercise, and be kept clean and healthy. This little girl and Cocoa will grow up together and be friends for a long, long time.

Note

The dog in the top photograph is a wirehaired dachshund like Max and Missy. But there are two other kinds of dachshunds as well: the long-haired dachshund (*middle*) and the shorthaired dachshund (*bottom*).